GREENHOUSE GARDENING

FOR BEGINNERS

TABLE OF CONTENTS

INTRODUCTION

Thank you for choosing Greenhouse Gardening for Beginners: The Complete Guide to Growing Vegetables, Fruits, Herbs, and Edibles Flowers in any Kind of Greenhouse.

Do you know you can extend the growing season by installing a greenhouse? With a greenhouse, you will be able to accomplish your goals almost every day of the year. Growing plants such as vegetables, fruits, herbs and so on in greenhouses allow for season extension, sometimes by months, offering you all year-round gardening opportunity. Even as you cannot grow all veggies in greenhouses twelve months of the year, you have the privilege to plant cold-weather vegetables and allow them growing through the nastiest of the winter climate by installing a simple heating system.

A greenhouse in your backyard will offer a stable, warm environment where plants grow faster and stronger than those grown in a traditional garden, as you would be creating a suitable atmosphere for them to flourish. You can also use it to get a jump start on the growing seasons, where you can sow plants such as peppers and tomatoes early and later move them to the garden. Whatsoever your motive for choosing a greenhouse, there are different types, modes, and costs for you to consider when wanting to start gardening.

This book provides you with adequate information on the easiest and the best ways to start and keep a productive and beautiful greenhouse of your dream.

Thanks again for choosing this book. I hope you find all the information helpful.

CHAPTER ONE

Planning and Building Greenhouse

Vegetables are fresher when they are from your own garden. Though "growing season" is usually between spring and autumn, you can extend the growing and harvesting of your crops anytime when growing in greenhouses. A greenhouse controls light, humidity, water, and temperature. The variety of vegetable you can grow in your greenhouse depends on the location and temperature of the structure. Opting for the right varieties to grow in the greenhouse is crucial for your overall garden's success. Here are some of the factors to consider when planning or building a greenhouse.

1. Site Selection

The closer is your greenhouse to your garden or home, the better. You also need to consider access to water and electricity as both of them are unavoidable. Find a level spot with optimum exposure to the sun. Find a place where your greenhouse will be receiving about six hours of direct sunlight daily through the winter. By orienting the greenhouse east to west, the biggest part will get full exposure to the southern sun. If you do not have an area with sufficient sunlight, you can add grow light. Deciduous trees will offer necessary shade during summer, and lose their leaves in the fall; this will give room for sun in the winter. Don't choose a location close to coniferous trees or any objects that would grow dim through the long winter months. Whichever surface you placed your greenhouse must allow adequate drainage.

2. Glazing

Glazing means covering around the frame of your greenhouse. This allows for absorption of sunlight and the heat while it keeps the elements out. The best glazing material is glass, but very costly. Double-glazed glass windows neutralize and absorb incoming sunlight. Plastic covers made of materials like acrylic, vinyl, polyethylene or fiberglass may be, lightweight, inexpensive, and absorb more sunlight, but might also quickly spoil and make heat to break out. Polycarbonate is cheaper than glass, light-weight, and holds heat well than both the plastic and glass. In addition, you can use polycarbonate on bent or flat surfaces, and it's very sturdy. However, any of the sources should be strong enough to protect against heavy snowfall and rainstorms

3. Accessories

Apart from the greenhouse frame, there are several accessories that fit in. Depending on your budget and commitment, you can add a potting bench, a tool rack, a fan, a heating system, a mist system, automatic vents, shelving and so on. Think about what you really need, what you would love to have, and what your greenhouse can contain.

CHAPTER TWO

Benefits of Greenhouse Gardening

Greenhouse gardening provides numerous benefits that go beyond what traditional gardening offers. Whether you opt for a simple greenhouse or more complex one, you'll still benefit from the numerous advantages. If you consider growing plants in a greenhouse, here are some of the many benefits to enjoy.

1. Extended Growing Season

One of the benefits of greenhouse gardening is that it provides you with an elongated growing season. You don't have many varied temperatures in a greenhouse, as the radiation of the sun is trapped in the enclosed space, keeping the heat inside the structure. You can extend the growing season, even in cold weather.

2. Grow a Wide range of Plants

You will be able to grow a wide range of plants when gardening with a greenhouse. It will give you the opportunity to experiment with uncommon and exotic plants in the local area.

3. Garden in Any Weather

Maintaining a garden in bad weather could be a problem. With a greenhouse, you have nothing to worry about as all your plants are sheltered. You can garden and keep dry even if it is raining outside.

4. Protection from Pests and Predators

Another great benefit of greenhouse gardening is that to a large extent, it protects plants from predators and pests. Predators such as squirrels, deer, and moles can be easily kept off. Tiny pests like rodents prevented by including screens and traps.

5. Provide Optimal Growing Environment

A greenhouse gardening will allow you to provide the perfect growing environment for any variety of plants you are growing – be it vegetables, fruits, flowers, herbs etc. Providing the best growing atmosphere helps you to improve your plant's growth, leaving you with healthier and optimum crops production.

6. Save Energy

Gardening in greenhouse offers you the benefit of saving energy. You can possibly preserve your sources of energy like water since you will have more control over these sources of energy which is contrary to traditional gardening.

7. Go Green with Your Greenhouse

Greenhouse gardening allows you to go green. This will benefit both you and the environs. Growing additional plants helps to present fresher and cleaner environment, making a greenhouse a perfect instrument for combating global warming.

8. Keep Beneficial Insects Inside

Some beneficial insects like ladybug can be easily kept within the greenhouse. They will help reduce the number of bad insects by eating them. However, these beneficial insects can easily leave the traditional garden.

9. Relaxation and Stress Relief

Greenhouse gardening gives the opportunity to relax and relieve stress. It presents an ideal place where you can catch fun while tending the plants.

Greenhouse gardening is not only about growing plants but has to do with living a more environmentally friendly life and changing one's lifestyle. It also has to do with teaching kids and family members to garden, since it's an important skill to learn and bring about family bonding.

CHAPTER THREE

Types of Greenhouse

A greenhouse is a structure where we can grow plants under controlled atmosphere. These buildings varied in size from small lean-to to very huge structures. Greenhouses can be with different kinds of covering materials like plastic or glass roof and often plastic or glass walls. Here are some examples of the greenhouse to consider for growing healthy plants.

1. Lean-to or Attached

An attached greenhouse saves you the stress of building all four walls. You will have at least one well-built weight-bearing wall on ground (be it your house or garage), so you can build the three sides of the greenhouse lighter. This structure is often cheaper than other models of greenhouse and perfect for growing seedling, herbs, and some veggies in locations where there is ample space. The shortcoming of the attached greenhouse is that only three sides will be receiving sunlight.

2. Freestanding

Freestanding greenhouse obviously stands alone, so you can situate them anywhere you want within your available space – as long as the location is level and gets sufficient sunlight. Though it's more costly than an attached greenhouse, the cost per plant is lower, as you can grow several more plants in it. With a freestanding greenhouse, you will have the privilege to begin planting earlier in the growing season (Jan or Feb) and then, when frost begins, you could take your plants in to extend the season through Oct or Nov. Freestanding greenhouse also serves as a shelter away from home. You can comfortably relax in it, while you'll be surrounded by the beauty of plants and flowers you grow.

3. Window-Mounted Greenhouse:

This type of greenhouse is mini and not expensive. It is solid, small, and can be placed outside a house window. A window-mounted greenhouse can be affixed to the window in such a way that there will be accessible from both in and outside. Whether attached to the exterior of the wall or used in place of the window. Usually, it contains about 3 or 4 shelves and widens only about a foot distant from the wall.

This type of greenhouse is most useful on east or south facing the wall and its warmness depends largely on the inner temperature of the building it is being affixed to.

4. Glazed Freestanding Greenhouse:

This type of greenhouse is basically similar to a freestanding model, but it is strictly made of plastic covering. Glazed greenhouses are considered as the cheapest but offer a large space for growing plants. The disadvantage of it is that it can spoil quickly and need regular maintenance all through seasonal changes and stormy weather. Nevertheless, it's significantly lightweight and keeps the required heat for plants to flourish.

Any of the above options produce brilliant greenhouse gardening and provides a means for sturdy, healthy plants all year round. Construct your greenhouse with strong, reliable materials like aluminum or untreated wood.

CHAPTER FOUR

Best Plants in Greenhouses

There is a considerable difference between the greenhouse vegetables and the crops grown as starter plants. Gardeners tend to grow fruits and vegetables in their greenhouse where they have the atmosphere to control temperature, extend the growing season, provide heat, and to protect them from frosting. Nevertheless, as a beginner to gardening and planting vegetables and fruits, you can choose among the following best veggies to grow in the greenhouse. Begin with easy vegetables that you can reap within a year, and then you can advance in the next season.

- **Chilies**

You can plant chilies right at your greenhouse corner. Either red or green varieties will grow well with other plants in your greenhouse, so the choice is yours.

- **Citrus fruits:**

Many winter fruits can be grown in your greenhouses – such as oranges, sweet and sour, melons, and lemons. They can survive even the coldest weather, so always make your winter evening a juicy one.

- **Coriander**

You don't want to miss out this refreshing leafy vegetable in the greenhouse garden. Coriander is an excellent topping for soups and salads. Provide adequate ventilation and water while the plant is growing, to optimize yield.

- **Cucumbers**

Cucumbers are of many varieties in different shapes and sizes. Whether eating raw pieces or cucumber salads, they are all delicious. You can easily grow them in your greenhouse. To retain cucumbers freshness, you'll need to do is to shrink-wrap them after harvest.

- **Grapes**

Most gardeners don't know they can grow grapes in the greenhouse. Grapes will strive in greenhouse once you guard them against pest and take proper care of the varieties such as "Buckland Sweetwater" and "black ham burgh".

- **Herbs**:

Greenhouse gardening is not complete without growing herbs as they are as suitable in roots and even without. You can improve your meal taste with the help of watercress, cilantro, basil, garlic, ginger, and more.

- **Leafy greens**

It is ideal to start with veggies that belong to "salad family" – Virtually all other leafy vegetable grows in a similar way, particularly when we talk about the bedding plants. We need adequate knowledge when growing leafy vegetables. They're different in colors and tastes. They can be an excellent source of income since you could sell them to different grocery stores.

- **Microgreens**

You can grow beautiful and delicious peas, radish, beets, tatsoi, Choi and so on. They are suitable for growing as a beginner to greenhouse gardening.

- **Peaches**

Peaches are also a good choice for the newbie to the greenhouse and small gardening. They are straightforward to grow and very nutritious.

- **Peppers**

Peppers make the dishes taste better. Any variety of peppers can be easily grown in the greenhouse as they have light to intensify taste and colors are fantastic.

- **Raspberries**

Raspberries are easy to grow, delicious, and make a perfect addition to your fruit salads. Also, you can make good money by growing and supplying raspberries to cake bakers.

- **Spinach**

Spinach is one the best plants for greenhouse – If you want to get tastiest and the freshest spinach, pick it from the garden and cook it straight away. It's highly nutritious that you can boost your intake of minerals and vitamins immediately. Most significantly, growing and keeping spinach is trouble-free.

- **Strawberries**

Start the season by filling your greenhouse with sweet fleshy strawberries. You can grow any variety, just ensure you give them adequate space and aeration.

- **Swiss chard and squash**

These two wonderful plants come in different varieties and they are straightforward to grow in a greenhouse. You will earn more income by selling them to grocery stores.

- **Tomatoes**

Tomatoes are also in many varieties, shapes, and colors. Any variety can be grown in a greenhouse for beginners - They're straightforward to maintain especially the beefsteak type.

The above are some of the best fruits and vegetable to begin your gardening. Greenhouse gardening is not just rewarding activity but also fun!

CHAPTER FIVE

Gardening Tools & Accessories

- **Pruner**

Sharp pruner is essential for tasks like harvesting tomatoes and clipping stems. It is a tool you will often need. In fact, most gardeners wear it on their belt to keep it nearby. Try to buy high-quality pruner that would serve for long.

- **Trowel**

A trowel is useful for digging small holes. Go for a handle that's firm in your hand and a good quality and affordable product.

- **Garden Fork**

Garden fork or digging fork is useful for turning the soil in existing or new beds, sifting out stones and breaking up clods. You will also need it for turning compost and in raised beds; it's useful for loosening and aerating soil before planting.

- **Gloves**

Every gardener must have one or two pair of nitrile-coated gloves as it presents great handiness and easy to wash. However, nitrile gloves are not good enough for chilly-weather gardening, thus you might have an additional pair of lined waterproof gloves.

- **Shovel**

You will need a traditional spade to turn soil on your vegetable garden. Do not neglect specialized shovels, such as a kombi shovel (with a pointed tooth suitable for digging in heavy clay) or sharp spading shovel (with a thin blade ideal for working on rocky soil and established beds) if they will be useful in your garden.

- **Hoe &Rake**

A hoe is a good tool for working soil and weeding, in vegetable gardening in particular. A standard curve rake is ideal for working soil and smoothing out beds before planting.

- **Watering Gear**

Choose a watering can that has a large opening and detachable. Choose a high-quality hose with adjustable hose nozzle and moderate 'shower' setting.

- **Wheelbarrow**

As a gardener, you'll need a wheelbarrow, garden cart or heavy-duty carriage to convey garden tools, plants, and bulk materials (such as mulch, compost, thick soil and so on) around the yard. Opt for a high-quality wheelbarrow that will last for years

- **Premium Quality Soil**

The success of any garden is to a large extent determined by the soil's quality. Opt for a premium mix that offers a rich, well-drained base, like potting mix.

CHAPTER SIX

Growing Plants in Greenhouse

1. How to Grow Vegetables

Choose the vegetables you want to grow based on the temperature of the greenhouse.

- **Choose the Best Variety**

Select the varieties of vegetables to grow in your greenhouse. “Cool season” veggies like lettuce and broccoli tend to thrive in a greenhouse with daylight temperature from fifty to seventy degrees F. and at nighttime from forty-five to fifty-five degrees F. “Cool season” plants don’t necessarily need hot direct sunlight. “Warm season” veggies like peppers and cucumbers will grow well in a greenhouse with a daytime temperature of sixty to eighty-five degrees F. and from fifty-five to sixty-five degrees F at night. "Warm season" veggies require bright light. "Warm and cool" varieties don't grow well collectively in the same greenhouse as their required temperature varied.

- **Sow the Plants or Seeds**

Put the vegetable plants or seeds into pots with about two-thirds full soil. Position the plants in a way that the tallest ones sit on shelves in the back of the greenhouse. Leave sufficient space between plants. Water your plants as necessary since indoor garden crops would not benefit from rainfall.

- **Install Thermometers**

Install two thermometers, each one for gauging the temperatures outdoors and indoors. When your greenhouse gets extremely hot indoors, open a door or window to help normalize the temperature by allowing some fresh air in. Insulate doors and windows if your greenhouse is losing heat.

- **Group Plants Together**

Plant companion crops together. Though "companion planting" isn't a new ideal, we cannot overemphasize its adoption in an organic greenhouse. Gardening in a greenhouse is not totally free from pests troubles, but the majority of it can be prevented naturally by the use of companion planting.

I. Plant garlic, bay leaf, spearmint or peppermint to ward-off those little critters.

II. An Elder shrub will prevent mice if plant directly into the ground.

III. Leeks and onions planted beside carrots prevent carrot fly.

IV. Nasturtiums drive out aphids.

V. French Marigolds close to tomatoes will discourage blackfly and greenfly.

VI. For slugs and snails, there is the well-known beer trap. The scent of the beer will attract them, once they sip it, they will get drunk and drown.

VII. However, to attract beneficial bugs, plant achillea, buddleia, and flowering herbs like lavender, rosemary, and dill through your greenhouse. These would draw pest-devouring hoverflies, lacewings, and ladybirds.

- **Plant with Organic Soil**

Make use of organic soil. Do not skimp on the soil quality or the organic additives you will add to your soil, such as manure, compost or sea products like kelp. Just like fertilizer, additives boost your soil's health. Keep in mind; additives differ, depending on the plants you are growing. Different plants with varied needs.

- **Provide Enough Space for Plants**

Watch out if you are growing taller fruits and vegetables like corn or tomatoes directly into the ground, ensure there is enough ceiling space for them to grow to their maximum height. Also, ascertain the soil is free from hazardous toxins and organisms. If you notice your soil has toxins, buy a "soil check" tool from a nursery.

- **Use Organic Compost**

Compost is the most crucial and most inexpensive component in your veggies garden. Ensure your compost remain organic. This implies that whatever you throw in there must be free of chemicals. If you toss in something that has chemicals into your compost bin, automatically, it would contain chemicals.

- **Prevent Weeds**

Take care of weeds before they grow. Place 1” to 2” width of newspaper on the soil’s top and cover with roughly the same quantity of mulch or soil. The thicker the paper, the more it would eliminate weed. Nearly all inks of the newspapers are soy-based so they won’t damage your little plants. Don’t make use of the shiny color inserts since they are very toxic and the glossy surface hinders water penetration.

However, plain old newspapers will work perfectly, and will also decompose after a while, thus serve as a healthy additive to your soil.

- **Use Organic Herbicides**

Identify your organic herbicides. If you experience excessive bug's infestation and you need to use an herbicide, it's ideal to use an organic soap mixture. Opt for the most affordable brand of lemon dish soap that is available. The less-expensive type will usually contain less toxic additives. Combine a tablespoon of the soap with one gallon of water and pour into a spraying device. Spray the bottom and the top of the leaves. Repeat the process weekly or bi-weekly. This soap mixture has the additional advantage of minimizing the menace of many diseases that could emerge.

- **Pull Spent Plants**

Pull used up plants from the ground. After harvesting your vegetables and fruits, pull the spent plants from the ground and throw them in your compost bin for the coming year's gardening. Pulling used up plants from the soil helps to deter pests and retain the soil's nutrients.

2. How to Grow Fruits

As most gardeners choose to grow varieties of vegetables in the greenhouse, veggies are definitely not the only available options. Even in an unheated greenhouse, a wide range of fruits such as lemons, peaches, and grapes can all be easily grown as well.

- **Grapes**

Most people thought vines always demand high temperatures, but with right variety selection, you'll have your own bounty of grapes." Buckland Sweetwater" and "Black Ham burgh" varieties, for example, are suitable for cool weather. However, with a heated greenhouse, you have several options available to you.

Vines need open, well-draining soil to thrive and it's essential to understand this aspect of their growing as drenched soil can have bad impacts on them. You will need to support young plants with stout canes as they become established. Vine crops produce their flowers and fruits on each new growth for the year, so you will need to prune the side-shoots produced through summer to their last bud (in the next winter) to encourage good crops.

You will need to pay attention to the plants over the year, supply them with adequate water, and high-quality fertilizer to keep them in a good state. As the fruits grow, you need to thin them with long scissors, so they will be able to grow bigger.

Unfortunately, vines are susceptible to a number of pests, such as scale insects, red spider mites, and aphids. Inspect the plants often and take rapid steps, the moment you notice a sign of threats. Mildew can also be a trouble to the fruits. However, with proper attention and little effort, you can provide a handful of bunches of your own grapes, even if you have a small greenhouse.

- **Citrus Fruits**

You can also grow oranges, lemons, and tangerines in a greenhouse. They only demand about 55 degrees

F temperature for the pips to sprout and would survive the winter, in as much as their environment stays above 40 degrees F. Though, it is easier to grow them from pips to produce your own trees, but not a quick process. It may take up to ten years before they start producing their fruits. With prompt propagation, fruits production will be a bit faster.

- **Nectarines and Peaches**

You can grow both nectarines and peaches in either cool or unheated greenhouses. In as much as you select the right variety. Nectarines variety such as "Pine Apple" and "Humboldt" are suitable for the unheated or cool greenhouse, they usually begin to ripen later in the season, produce fruits in Sept and regularly into Oct. For peaches, "Peregrine" is a good choice, start ripening in August and it's self-fertile.

Keeping the trees in good condition is easy with little efforts and time. Once they produce fruits, you need to prune them to keep a fan shape. This will give the fruits enough space to grow well and makes picking them hitch-free.

Nectarines and peaches grown in the greenhouse usually have compact roots, thus the need to frequently water and feed them with fertilizer through the growing season. Once the trees have been founded, the plants will need some help since pollinating insects are not present in the greenhouse. Throughout the plants flowering period, you will need to be transferring pollen from flower to flower on a daily basis, using a tiny brush. Also, to create the best success opportunity, you will need to increase the greenhouse's moisture. Once the fruits have grown to about walnuts size, you may need to thin them

3. How to Grow Herbs

Growing herbs in greenhouses jump-start the garden season for the winter-weary and it's cheaper than purchasing mature garden plants. You can start perennial herbs in the greenhouse with plugs or plant cutting, annual and biennial herbs with seeds.

The methods of growing herbs in the greenhouse are similar to growing vegetables. However, there are some applications mainly for herbs planting. And all herbs are not with the same growing requirements. Rosemary, for example, is best grown in single containers in moderately fertile soil, while mint will thrive in well-raised greenhouse beds.

Some herbs like coriander and chervil are best to be planted in autumn and will flourish in winter in a frost-free greenhouse. Chervil especially thrives in a greenhouse during winter in partial shade or sun and well-drained soil.

In addition, you can plant root cuttings from chervil in mid-winter to enjoy its constant culinary purpose. You can also grow coriander for leaves or seeds all through the year, provided it's in well-drained, fertile, and lightweight soil, in partial shade for leaf growth and full sun for seed production.

Herbaceous perennial herbs like dill, thyme, tarragon, and chives grown outside in cool weather can be moved to a greenhouse in winter. Carefully transplant the plants into high-quality potting-mix before frost. Give them the necessary attention, and you will continue to enjoy fresh culinary fare all through the winter months.

Most herbs enjoy the protection of greenhouses, even if you are not intending to harvest them in winter. Parsley, lemon verbena, cumin, and anise, for instance, can be moved into the greenhouse in cool weather, and have their plants covered with a cloche or shoots and roots wrapped in plastic.

Gardeners who cultivate herbs in pots outside can also move in their containers into a heated greenhouse to preserve them for the winter.

Growing plants in greenhouses aren't free from challenges, getting the right conditions, preventing the ravage of diseases and pests - even raising the plants correctly - may all need some efforts to succeed, but in the end, you could happily walk to your garden and pick your own grown food!

CHAPTER SEVEN

Greenhouse Environmental Control

- **Heating**

If you reside in frosty weather it is necessary you insulate your greenhouse to keep your plants toasty warm. When your plants receive enough sun through the day, an un-insulated greenhouse would quickly cool off at night. This is why a heating system is required. You can opt for solar heaters designed specifically for the greenhouse, or small gas heaters designed to be fixed through a masonry wall, or a 220-volt circuit electric heater. All of them work well. Soil heating cables beneath beds coupled with radiant heat lamps hang over plants will keep most plants adequately warm. Ensure your greenhouse is vented and always remember to shut-off any of your automatic heating systems.

Tip: Put barrels of water or rocks inside your greenhouse to retain the sun's heat and keep plants warm through the cold evening.

- **Shading**

In a hot environment or if the sunlight is directly hitting the greenhouses, shade will protect the plants from being burnt by lessening the sum of summer sun. Vinyl plastic shading, roll-up screens of wood or aluminum, or painted on objects can all be used to shade plants.

- **Ventilation**

Even in the cold climate plants can get too hot, therefore ventilation is vital to a good greenhouse. You can get temperature an electric-sensitive hydraulic vents that open and close automatically. You can hand crank vent, but it's crucial to monitor the temperature closely. You can install an oscillating fan to help keep air circulating the greenhouse and avert diseases outbreak.

- **Floor Materials**

The greenhouse floor can be made of many materials such as metal grates, flagstone, wood decking, and gravel, or uncovered. However, you can only leave the floor uncovered if your yard stays bone-dry, if not it will turn a murky swamp. A gravel floor drains well, economical, and could be simply renewed by putting additional gravel.

- **Pests**

The first step in preventing pest problems is keeping your gardening equipment and greenhouse clean. Carefully Inspect plants before taking them into your greenhouse to ascertain they are free of bugs and diseases. Take out any plants with diseases or bugs. Spray plant flora with mild insect killing soap to deter or kill various soft-bodied pests. Encourage beneficial bugs such as spider mite predators, whitefly parasites, green lacewings, and ladybugs as they eat bad bugs.

CHAPTER EIGHT

Watering Plants and Irrigation in Greenhouse

Watering systems in the greenhouse are vital aspects of creating the ultimate growing environment. Generally, plants grown in a closed environment like greenhouses require more attention and care than traditional garden plants. Outdoors plants automatically receive water each time it rains. However, the plants in your greenhouse solely depend on you for watering. When watering your greenhouse plants, you ought to be familiar with the level of moisture in your greenhouse and the water requirement of each variety of plants.

- The ideal time to water your greenhouse plants is early in the morning or late in the evening when we usually experience the lowest temperature.
- Make your watering method perfect. Water plants in greenhouses with a simple stream of water such as the supplied from a watering can. Water can splash with high pressure. Causing spreads of diseases and promoting soil fungi's growth.
- Also when watering, do not flood your plants at once. Rather spray them little by little and allow each batch to soak into the soil before re-applying. Once water starts running out of the pot base, stop watering.
- Let your plants dry off. Though some plants that require damp soil, mostly flourish when

you allow their soil to dry out. Rather than watering your plants one or two times daily, wait till the top two inches of the soil are dried up (except the plants require otherwise). Since the level of the greenhouse moisture is so high. You can easily over-water your plants in greenhouses.

- Keep your mind on the season. You will need to water greenhouse plants more often in summer than in spring or fall, so inspect the soil more frequently. The required water of most plants somewhat reduces in winter. Moreover, a humid cool environment in a greenhouse could cause the growth of fungus.

Greenhouse Irrigation:

Water for greenhouses can be run through a drip system or pipe or even piped in professionally. Any technique you may adopt, the creation of flow amounts, zones, timing, and mode of delivery are all aspect of irrigation in greenhouses.

Simple Watering System

Greenhouse watering method might be merely a simple hose and some sprayers or urbane underground plumbed works. Hand watering and running water through the pipe is straightforward but can be tedious. Capillary mats are a simple technique to use. You only put them beneath your flats and pots and pour out water bit by bit, which the container's drip holes take up to the roots of the plants. This method is referred to as sub-irrigation, which lessens evaporation and prevents overwatering that can encourage fungal diseases and rots. The surplus water will go to a flood floor or the plastic liners that will direct the water back into the structure to be reused for watering plants in other drip lines in the greenhouse.

Drip Greenhouse Irrigation

Not every plant demands the same frequency and amount of water. Under or over-watering can lead to plants health troubles. To avoid this situation, set up a simple irrigation scheme that you can use to run smaller or larger flows of water directly to flats or pots. This type of water can be regulated for a greenhouse with a flow gauge or timer. The system starts with a baseline and then peripheral feeder's lines. There is micro-tubing between each feeder line, run directly to the plants at the root line of the soil. The micro-tubing can be added or reduced as required and spray heads or drip can be used to supply the needed amount of water by each plant. This system is cheap and straightforward to adopt for watering plants in greenhouses.

CHAPTER NINE

Scheduling Plants for Year-Round Growing

You can use a productive greenhouse for most of the year. Heated greenhouses offer the greatest year-round use.

- **Late winter to early spring**

Sow hardy crops such as peas, onions, lettuce, early leeks, celeriac, cabbage, and Brussels sprouts for planting out when the hot climate arrives. They will germinate with the help of heater propagator. You can sow peppers, tomatoes, and other tender plants early in a propagator in heated greenhouses.

- **Mid-spring**

Sow fast-growing tender plants like sweet corn, melons, French beans, cucumbers, pumpkins, squashes, and courgettes so they will be ready to plant in their permanent locations in the greenhouse in late spring. They will germinate with the help of heated propagator. Sow basil for growing on indoors or moving outdoors in summer. Purchase ready-grown tomato and pepper plants to introduce to an unheated greenhouse.

- **Late spring to early summer**

Plant summer greenhouse plants into their final positions indoors Harden off and plant out young plants of outdoor crops once the frost has passed

- **Mid-summer**

Pick summer crops, Pull used up melon, French bean or cucumber (you can replace them with later sown plants). Sow parsley, French bean, and Calabrese outdoors for taking in when summer crops have finished

- **Late summer**

If you have enough space, sow baby carrots, spicy salad leaves, and lettuces indoors to take advantage of the autumn sun and provide late harvests. In a heated greenhouse, plant new potatoes for Christmas crops.

- **Autumn**

Take out spent summer crops. Sow parsley, French bean, and Calabrese seedling to mature indoors. Grow lettuces in grow bags or beds outside to harvest over winter. Grow peas and broad beans to over-winter and be planted outside early in spring. Plant pea shoots and hardy lettuces cultivars to be picked indoors in spring

CHAPTER TEN

Harvesting and Storing Your Bounties

Harvesting bounty like all gardening is not difficult, but after you must have put all your effort and time into fruitfully growing your crops, you want to ensure you're harvesting at the appropriate time for best taste and excellent storage. The following tips will be of help.

Tips for Harvesting Vegetables:

1. Bigger isn't always the best

A lot of vegetables is at their crest of tenderness and quality when still young. For example beans, cucumbers, potatoes, peas, turnips, and zucchini. Others, like watermelons and tomatoes, are best to pick when completely ripe.

2. **Avoid wet weather**

Vegetable gardeners know the importance of the plants to get regular moisture. However, it's best not to harvest crops when it is raining, particularly disease-prone crops such as beans, cucumbers, squash, and tomatoes. Also, avoid working these plants in moist weather

3. **Harvest often**

People who grow zucchini can tell you that a little fruit can go from two-inch to two two-feet within a few days. Consequently, it is ideal to stay on top of harvesting. Frequent picking will lead to larger yield, good-quality, and better-tasting vegetables.

4. Use proper tools

Form some veggies like kale, lettuce, peas, beans etc, harvesting devices are not necessary. But for certain crops such as carrots, cucumbers, potatoes, large-fruited tomatoes, and zucchini, it is ideal to use a garden fork, pruning shears, sharp knife, or other tools to prevent plant or the harvested fruits damage. The damaged plant gives an avenue for diseases to enter, and fruits such as tomatoes or zucchini can bruise easily which would reduce eating quantity and storage. Put harvested veggies in a handy garden colander or basket for easy washing and to prevent damage.

- **Beans**

Beans can be harvested up until frost begins.

Snap Beans

Yellow, green come in both pole and bush varieties.

Pods should be hard and crispy at harvest. They should crack if you smash one in half. The seeds in it ought to be small and immature since beans are over-matured when the seeds have started to fill out the pods. Grip the pod with one hand and the stem using the other to prevent removing branches that would produce later more pickling. Use a scissors or your finger to gently pinch the pods. To keep plants productive, pick all pods.

Shell Beans

Soybeans, Lima, Fava, Romano, Southern Peas, and so on - come in pole bush and bush varieties

Harvest shell beans varieties when the pods change color and the seed are completely formed but not dry off. Pods should be chubby, solid, and tender. The beans quality reduces if left on the plant for too long. To keep the plants productive, harvest every few days. For both snap and shell beans, the pods can be kept in plastic bags for one to two weeks in the refrigerator, or frozen.

Dried Beans

Pinto, Navy, Great Northern, etc. - come in both pole and bush varieties

Allow the pods to dry as possible in the plant, harvest dry beans pods when they've turned brown and the seeds are very firm. You can hear the ratting of the seeds inside the pods. In too moist weather for the beans to dry, pick the pods and hang them inside.

Pods will split willingly when completely dried, making it easy to remove the seeds. Shell the beans when fully dried, and put in a sealed jar, store in dry, cool place for up to one year.

- **Broccoli**

Broccoli is ready to harvest when heads are deep green, still firm, and flowers begin to open out. If buds begin to divide and the yellow petals in begin to show, harvest with right away. Cut the stems at a slant around four to six inches beneath the head. Getting rid of the head on some varieties would produce side shoots in the leaves axils and you can get four to six cuttings of shoots in a plant over a number of weeks. The leaves are tough but can be used in stews and soups. The thick stems are edible, but peel them before use. Soak your broccoli's heads in a salt water mixture (one or two tablespoons of salt in a gallon3.8 liter of water) for twenty to thirty minutes before storing or cooking. This would eliminate any cabbageworms hiding in the head. You can keep broccoli in the refrigerator for a week or more, provided it's wrapped in plastic. The ideal method of storing broccoli for a long time is by blanching and freezing.

- **Cabbage**

Green and Red

Cabbage is good to be harvested when the head is full and firm. Use a sharp knife to cut the stalk at the head base and remove the surface leaves. The ideal time to harvest cabbage is morning when heads are calm. After you have removed the centre head, small heads might emerge where the bottom leaves connect the stem. Allow them to spout and you will have one more head weighing about one to two pounds.

After the center head has been removed, small heads may develop where the base leaves meet the stem. Let one of them grow and you'll often get another head weighing around 1 or 2 pounds (.5-.9 kg). Keep heads in a cold, moist area, just about freezing and around 90% humidity.

- **Carrots**

  Carrots are usually good for harvest in two to three months or when they have reached the size you want. Pull one or two plants to check the size. Use a fork to loosen the soil and softly pull them from the soil. Watering prior to harvest will make it easier to pull them out. Remove soil from them and twist off the tops. Carrot can be left in the ground until they are needed as the matured ones would preserve their quality in the soil except the weather becomes very hot. Following the first hard frost, but you will need to harvest all your carrots before ground freezes

- **Cucumbers**

We grow varieties of cucumbers in different sizes and shapes. Nevertheless, all of the cucumber types offer the utmost quality harvest and best-tasting when picked young. For round verities like crystal apple, dragon's egg, or lemon, collect when the fruits are pale green and about 1½ to 3 inch long. For long-fruited varieties, follow the direction in the seed catalog to harvest the plants. However, you can also harvest them young as cucumbers are super crisp and less bitter when picked young.

- **Eggplants**

It could be difficult to eggplants is to be harvested and picking over-mature, they would be seedy and bitter. We have many types of eggplants with different color, shapes, and sizes, but, usually picked when the fruits are a bit smaller than signified in the seed catalog and the seed is glossy. Use garden shears or sharp pair of pruners to cut eggplants from the plants and put in a basket to prevent bruising

- **Lettuce**

Leaf Lettuce

Leaf lettuce matured within forty days of the seedling. Begin to harvest once the leaves are large enough to consume, about four to five inches long. The large outer leaves can be picked or cut the whole plant off about one inch over the ground, to give room for new plant growth that will get to edible size in the next three to five weeks. Pick leaf lettuce in the morning when the leaves are crispy and fully moist. Harvest the whole plant if your crop is susceptible to a hard frost or begins to bolt.

Head Lettuce

Head and romaine lettuce matured about seventy days from seeds and twenty to thirty-five days from transplants. Pick by cutting the plant to the level of the ground when the head is solid. For crispy lettuce, pick in the morning and consume the same day. However, you can refrigerate most lettuce for about one to two weeks. Iceberg lettuce keeps up to three weeks.

- **Melons**

It is ideal to allow melon to ripe on the vine. Picking them when ripen is vital for you to get the best flavor as the plants produce the fruits with a lot of natural sugar within a few days of ripening. Most store-purchased melons do not taste as sweet since they are ripened off the vine.

Muskmelons are ripening once the skin is russet instead of green between the outside netting. Most would have a strong melon scent, the crack that appears on the stem close to the attaching point with the melon signifies that the fruit is ready. This crack signifies that the fruit will fall off the vine in a few days, with little pressure.

- **Onions**

Onions are good to be harvested once they get to a usable size. All the same, your cue to begin the harvesting process when the leaves turn brown at the edges or start to flop over. Use a garden fork to cautiously dig them out of the soil. Spread the bulbs on the surface of the soil, or on a cable rack for proper ventilation.

Curing Onions

You will need to 'cure' onions before storing them. This simply implies fully drying the outer skins. Drying can be done by moving your onions under cover. You could dry onions on layers of newspaper or racks in a cold frame or hoop house, This can also be done for other alliums like garlic and shallots. Spread out the onions very well and ensure there is enough ventilation to prevent mold or rotting and wick away wetness. It may take about two weeks for onions to fully dry off. They can be stored once the leaves are fully shriveled, the skins are papery, and the roots are sinewy and dry. Cut off the roots at this point and take out any loose skin.

Storing Onions

Store your onions in a cool, dry, airy space without direct sunlight. An unheated room in the house or garage is appropriate. Use any soft bulbs or thick-necked onions as soon as possible. You can put Individual onions in netting sacks or veggie storage nets and hang them up off the ground. Inspect the nets from time to time and take out any spoilt onions

- **Peas** (Snap and Snow)

Peas are ready to pick roughly three weeks after they have sprout flowers. The best way to test for their ripeness is to pick a pod from the vine and taste. For snap peas, begin to harvest once the pods have become crisp and plump. For snow peas, begin to pick once the pods are formed, but the fruit in it is still small. Pick early in the morning when the pods are crispy for longer freshness and better storage. Uproot the plant, or carefully pull them off, or cut the pods from the plants with scissors. Harvest daily to keep high production and stop pods turning stringy and tough.

- **Sweet Peppers**

Nearly all varieties of sweet peppers would turn from green to red, purple, orange, or yellow as they mature. Peppers can be harvested while they still fully grown and green, or leave them for one or two more weeks to color up and get to the peak of its flavor and sweetness. Use pruning shears clip the fruits from the plants to avoid damages.

- **Tomatoes**

Tomatoes are ready to harvest when they change color. For finest flavor, pick tomatoes when hard and completely colored. For large-fruited tomatoes like those with purple or black color, check the pictures in the seed catalog to have the idea of when to pick them. Nevertheless, if you harvest tomatoes before ripen; leave it for a few more days in your kitchen to ripen.

For best storage, tomatoes are best to store at room temperature. Don't refrigerate tomatoes as cool temperatures make them lose texture and flavor.

- **Turnips**

Turnips grow quickly and offer both edible foliage and tasty roots. Start harvesting the salad varieties, such as 'Hakurei ' when roots are about one inch across. Keep harvesting roots regularly as those left for long in the soil would turn woody. Since turnips are quick growers, plant successive crops every few weeks to keep an extensive harvest of high-quality roots.

- **Zucchini**

Zucchini would be at their firmest and tastiest when harvested immature – about four to six inches long for the longer types or 1½ to 3 inches across for pattypan varieties. Use a pair of pruner or sharp knife to slice the fruits from the plant and put in a basket to avoid damage.

BONUS!

15 of the Most Common and Destructive Vegetable Garden Pest

Every veggies gardener faces pest troubles periodically, and managing the menace of these stubborn pests without using artificial chemical pesticides is an important stride in a healthy, fruitful garden. The below info will help you not only in managing 15 of the most common and destructive vegetable garden pest, but also to control veggie garden plants pests as a whole.

- **Pest Name**: Aphids (different species)

They are a familiar vegetable garden pest.

You can find aphids assembled in small groups on various vegetable plants, like lettuce and cabbage.

Identification: Aphids are tiny, pear-figure insects. They could be black, grey, red, brown, yellow, or green. Depending on their life stage and species, there are non-winged and winged aphids.

Susceptible Plants: They feed on several species of possible host veggie plants, such as cabbage, kale, lettuce, and tomatoes by sucking plant juices, causing growth deformation.

Prevention: Encourage helpful predatory insects by planting a large number of small flowers, flowering plants in the garden.

Organic product methods: Use neem-based insecticides, insecticidal soap, or horticultural oil to eliminate aphid infestations.

Physical methods: Aphids can be removed from plants by spraying them off using a sharp flow of water from the hose. You can also hand-picked them.

- **Pest Name**: Asparagus beetle

Scientific Name: Crioceris Asparagi

Asparagus beetles are a familiar pest for asparagus planters.

Adults of Asparagus beetle are very distinct.

Identification: asparagus beetles adults are black with a red mark light behind their head and creamy yellow spots in their body. The larvae are army-green.

Susceptible Plants: They feed only on asparagus plants by chewing their ferns and spear.

Prevention: Cut down asparagus plant's ferns and clear out their fallen leaves in the autumn.

Organic Product Methods: Use neem-based insecticides, insecticidal soap, or horticultural oil to eliminate asparagus beetles.

Physical Control Methods: Remove the larvae from the plants every day with a mild broom – spider and helpful insect would find and eat them once on the ground. Shield the rising spears with floating row cover all through the harvesting season. Search for the little, dark eggs and remove them with hand.

- **Pest Name**: Cabbage Worms

Scientific Name: Artogeia rapae

Cabbageworm caterpillars are familiar pests of vegetable gardens and are very destructive.

Identification: They are light green colored with a dim yellow streak at the rear. Adult cabbage worms are white to yellowish-white butterflies with about 4 black spots on their wings.

Susceptible Plants: All members of the cabbage family, such as radish, Brussels sprouts, kohlrabi, turnip, kale, cauliflower, and broccoli can be affected by cabbage worms. They chew holes in flower clusters and leaves.

Prevention: Hang bird-houses in the garden as birds like consuming caterpillars.

Organic Product Methods: Hot pepper wax, spinosad, and Bacillus thuringiensis (BT)-based insecticides are all powerful eliminators of cabbage worms.

Physical Control Methods: Shield vulnerable plants with floating row cover from planting to harvest time. You can also hand-pick caterpillars.

- **Pest Name**: Carrot Rust Fly

Scientific Name: Psila Rosae

Carrot rust fly creates tunnels through carrots and other root crops when eating.

Identification: The larvae of carrot rust flies are tiny, light brown maggots. The adult is very small, gleaming black with orange legs and head.

Susceptible Plants: Adult rust flies lay eggs close to various vegetable plants such as carrots, parsnips, celery, parsley, celeriac, and others. The larvae eat plant roots, leaving tunnels and scarring behind.

Preventions: Carrot rust flies are poor fliers, thus practice crop rotation each season. Wait until late May or early June before planting carrots as that is their off mating cycle.

Organic Product Methods: Release nematodes into the soil close to the carrot plant helps in controlling larvae. Use in the spring and follow the package direction.

Physical Control Methods: Protect carrots and other vulnerable plants with floating row cover from planting to harvest time. Female flies locate their host plants by smell, so inter-plant carrot with other crops like chives, garlic, and onions will help reduce carrot flies egg-laying.

- **Pest Name**: Colorado potato beetle

Scientific Name: Lepinotarsa decemlineata

The larvae feed on potatoes, potatoes leaves, tomatoes, and other garden plants.

Identification: The larvae of potato beetles are ½" plump, burgundy with rows of black spots on the side. Adults are 1/3" long, round with black and russet streaked wing covers.

Susceptible Plants: The potential hosts are all members of the tomato family such as potatoes, tomatoes, tomatillos, peppers, and eggplants. Both larvae and adult Colorado beetles damage plants all the way down to the leaf veins.

Preventions: Clear out the garden and practice crop rotation every season.

Organic Product Methods: Neem-based insecticides and spinosad-based organic sprays work perfectly.

Physical Control Methods: Hand-squish both the larvae and the adult. Protect the plants with floating row cover from planting to harvest time.

- **Pest Name**: Cucumber beetles

Scientific Name: Acalymma vittata

These beetles spread bacterial wilt diseases as they feed.

Identification: Cucumber beetles are of two species. They are generally light-yellow, one has black spots, while the other with black stripes. The larvae reside underground and can be hardly seen.

Susceptible Plants: The potential hosts are all members of the cucumber family like cucumbers, squash, gourds, pumpkins, and melons. You can also occasionally find them on beans, beets, corn, and other vegetables. Adult beetles create tiny shabby holes in the flowers and leaves and spread bacterial wilt disease.

Prevention: Grow only cucumber-resistant plants or bacterial wilt-resistant varieties like muskmelons, 'Saladin', 'Gemini' cucumber, 'Little leaf 19', and, butternut-type squashes since they are attacked by the beetles.

Organic Product Methods: Spray with spinosad-based insecticides as it's a power eliminator of cucumber beetles.

Physical Control Methods: Shield your plants with floating row cover and take away the cover once the plants sprout to flowers to give room for pollination. Mulch vulnerable plants using loose materials such as hay or straw to stop laying of eggs.

- **Pest Name**: Cutworms (different species)

There are destructive pests of the vegetable garden.

Cutworms chomp off plant stems at ground-level.

Identification: Cutworms larvae caterpillars are about 2” long and coil into a taut C-shape when troubled. The caterpillars mostly reside in the top few inches of the soil. Depending on the species, they can be gray, brown, yellow, or green.

Susceptible Plants: All young seedlings are vulnerable, but most affected are cabbage, kale, broccoli, tomatoes, and others. They chew seedlings or plant stems at ground level or chomp-off the outer stem tissues. An obvious sign of cutworms is the presence of severed or wilted seedling.

Prevention: Crop rotation is essential to protect the stems of young sprouts at their base. Exposing pupae to cold and predation by tilling the garden in autumn will also help.

Organic Product Methods: Mix beneficial nematodes (Heterorhabdtis bacterophora or Steinermema carpocapsae) with water and apply to the soil. It is very effective for eliminating cutworms.

Physical Control Methods: Bait cutworms with wheat bran or cornmeal paced in sunken bowls close to vulnerable plants. Caterpillars are attracted to grains but can't digest them, so they eventually die.

- **Name**: Flea beetles (different species)

Flea beetles are familiar pests for the vegetable garden. They can be tiny but could cause severe damages to radishes, eggplants, and other vegetable plants.

Identification: Very small, brown or black beetles, they are 1/10" long. Flea beetle moves very fast and jumps like a flea.

Susceptible Plants: Flea beetles are hostile to several plants, but most affected are eggplants, corn, brassicas, tomatoes, potatoes, and radishes. Flea beetles larvae reside underground and could eat plants roots. The adults create small, round holes in plants.

Prevention: Crop rotation is helpful.

Organic Product Methods: Add beneficial nematodes to the soil to help eliminate larvae. For adult flea beetles, use spinosad, kaolin clay, hot pepper, garlic oil, and neem-based products.

Physical Control Methods: Put yellow sticky cards over plants tops to trap adult flea beetles. Don't use floating row, it could trap newly appear flea beetles beneath it.

- **Pest Name**: Leaf miners (many species)

Leaf miners leave behind damaged plants

Identification: Adult leaf miners are ordinary flies that don't consume foliage. Their tiny, green or brown larvae eat the plant tissues.

Susceptible Plants: Various species of leaf miners feed on various plants, but common host plants are blueberries, nasturtiums, beets, chard, and spinach. Leaf miners larvae burrow between the tissue of the leaf, leaving lines and tunnels on leaves.

Prevention: Cut off those leaves that have tunnels all through the season and throw them away to avoid another generation.

Organic Product Methods: Leaf miners are difficult to control with products as their larvae are within the layers of leaves tissues. Spinosad and neem-based products can be effective to some extent.

Physical Control Methods: Protect the vulnerable plants with a floating row to prevent adults from having access to them. Plant plenty of flowering herbs in your garden to encourage helpful insects to assist in controlling the leaf miners.

- **Pest Name**: Mexican bean beetles

Scientific name: Epilachna varivestis

These bean beetles larvae feed on many varieties of beans.

The Mexican bean beetle is one of the familiar veggies garden pests.

Identification: Larvae of Mexican bean beetles are bright-yellow with mild, bristly spines. Adults are copper-colored, ladybug-like beetles with sixteen black spots.

Susceptible Plants: All types of beans such as soy, Lima, runner, pole, snap, and green could accommodate bean beetle and its larvae. The larvae and adults eat leaf tissue down to the veins. They also consume flowers and bean intermittently. You can find the larvae underneath the leaf.

Prevention: Cultivate a lot of flowering herbs since they encourage predator wasps that consume the larvae of bean beetles.

Organic Control Method: Mexican bean beetles can be controlled with spinosad and hot pepper wax. They are both effective.

Physical control Methods: Protect bean plants using floating row cover from the sprouting to flowering periods.

Pest Name: Snails and slugs (different species)

Slugs are one of the most reviled veggies garden pests.

Identification: Snail and slugs are not insects, soil-dwelling-mollusks. Slugs don't have shell, snails do. They could be mottled, brown, orange, black, gray, or tan and often leave a slime trail behind.

Susceptible Plants: A vegetable garden pest's guide without snails and slugs is not complete since almost every young seedling is host to the two pests. Snails and slugs feed on many varieties of vegetables and plants. They leave abnormal holes in leaf centers or margins. They feed on rainy days or at night; you hardly notice them in the day time.

Prevention: Water only in the morning since snails and slugs choose to feed on wet plants. Promote toads, frogs, and birds in the garden as they all eat snails and slugs.

Organic control methods: Make use of slug bait with iron phosphate active ingredient, don't use bait produced from methocarb or metaldehyde as they are poisonous to pets and other wildlife.

Physical control methods: Hand-pick snails or slugs and drop them into a container of soapy water.

- **Pest Name**: Squash bugs

Scientific Name: Anasa tristis)

Squash bugs are familiar pests in the vegetable garden.

They mate and lay bronze-colored eggs which will transform into more leaf-chewing squash bugs

Identification: A vegetable garden pest guide is not complete without mentioning what's most likely the strongest vegetable pest to eradicate. Adult squashes are 5/8' long, dark brown with flat egg-shaped body. The nymphs are gray with no wings. Squash bug usually feeds in groups. They also lay eggs in groups.

Susceptible Plants: Squash bugs affect all members of cucumber family like squash, pumpkins, cucumbers, melons, and zucchini. Nymphs and adults suck plant juices. Affected leaves turn yellow and die eventually.

Prevention: Practice crop rotation, plant resistant varieties, and keep the growing vines above the ground with the help of trellises.

Organic Product Methods: Neem or soap insecticides work well on nymphs, but products do not work well for adults.

Physical Control Methods: Protect the susceptible plants with floating row cover from planting time until flowering starts. Take out egg clusters every day with a piece of tape. Ensure you check underneath of leaves because that's where they often lay eggs.

- **Pest Name**: Squash vine bores

Scientific Name: Melittia satyriniformis

Squash vine borers adults lay eggs at the squash plants bottom. They are rarely seen.

Identification: Larvae of squash vine borers are plump, white caterpillars are found in the squash vine base. Adults are black and red moths that resemble big wasps.

Susceptible Plants: Every cucumber family members are vulnerable, including winter and summer squash, gourds, melons, and pumpkins. Cucumbers are seldom affected. Rapid plant's wilting is an obvious sign of the presence of borers. To confirm, search for holes in the stem tissue close to the ground.

Prevention: enclose a stripe of aluminum foil around the plant base, immediately after the main leaves emerge to guard the plant base against egg-laying females.

Organic Product Methods: Spray the base of stem weekly with insecticidal soap to choke any eggs. Also, use a needle-less syringe to inject the borer hole with Bacillus Thuringiensis (BT).

Physical Control Methods: Protect plants from planting to flowering time using a floating row cover. If you find borers' hole before the plant dies, slice the stem to open, remove the borer, and enclose the cut using a heap of soil.

- **Pest Name**: Tobacco/Tomato hornworms

Scientific Name: Manduca sexta, Manduca quinquemaculata)

These hornworms are very destructive pests to the vegetable garden.

Identification: Hornworm caterpillars are green with white stripes and spike stick or soft horn sticking out from their posteriors.

Susceptible Plants: All tomato family members such as tobacco, tomatoes, eggplants, peppers, and potatoes are host plants. They feed on plants leaves, often in the direction of the plants top. The caterpillars feed at night and reside in plants in the day time.

Prevention: Plant plenty of small flowers, flowering herbs close to the vulnerable plants. The flowers will draw small parasitic cotesia wasps that will eliminate hornworms.

Organic Control Methods: The best method of control is to hand-pick hornworms. If you are to use spray products, spinosad and Bacillus Thuringlensis (BT) are better.

Physical Controls Methods: Check plants for hornworms regularly and hand-pick

- **Pest Name**: Whiteflies

Scientific Name; Trialeurodes vaporariorum

Whiteflies are annoying vegetable garden pests that suck plant juices and cause distorted growth.

Identification: Whiteflies are small flies that look like a moth. Infected plants are usually covered with the flies' clammy honeydew excrement. Whiteflies are mostly gathering in crowds underneath the leaf.

Susceptible Plants: Common veggie plants that host whiteflies include citrus, peppers, tomatoes, sweet potatoes, and the rests. The nymphs and adults whitefly suck plant juices, resulting in wilt, yellow leaves, weak plants, and leaves drop in a severe case.

Prevention: Cautiously check for whiteflies in all new plants before buying from a plant sales outlet. This is a useful idea to prevent every one of the insects discussed in this chapter.

Organic Product Methods: Hot pepper wax, neem, horticultural oil, and insecticidal soap are all effective for controlling whitefly.

Physical Control Methods: Hang yellow sticky cards over the tops of the plant to arrest the adult flies and avert new generation.

A vegetable garden pest guide isn't complete without mentioning how inter-planting vegetable plants with annuals and flowering herbs could help reduce pests by attracting different species of helpful insects that feed on garden pests.

Printed in Great Britain
by Amazon

58658254R00064